DOMESTIC DOGS

DACHSHUNDS

by Susan H. Gray

Published in the United States of America by The Child's World®
1980 Lookout Drive • Mankato, MN 56003-1705
800-599-READ • www.childsworld.com

PHOTO CREDITS

© Andrzej Grygiel/epa/Corbis: 27
© blickwinkel/Alamy: 19
© David McGill/Alamy: 23
© iStockphoto.com/DigitalJoe: 25
© iStockphoto.com/John Long: cover, 1
© iStockphoto.com/ronibgood56: 11
© iStockphoto.com/stocksnapper: 21
© Mark Raycroft/Minden Pictures: 9, 13
© plainpicture GmbH & Co. KG/Alamy: 17
© Robert Recker/zefa/Corbis: 29
© SW Productions/Brand X/Corbis: 15

ACKNOWLEDGMENTS

The Child's World®: Mary Berendes, Publishing Director;
Katherine Stevenson, Editor

The Design Lab: Kathleen Petelinsek, Design and Page Production

LIBRARY OF CONGRESS CATALOGING-IN-PUBLICATION DATA

Gray, Susan Heinrichs.
  Dachshunds / by Susan H. Gray.
    p. cm. — (Domestic dogs)
  ISBN-13: 978-1-59296-964-7 (library bound : alk. paper)
  1. Dachshunds—Juvenile literature. I. Title.
  SF429.D25G68 2008
  636.753'8—dc22   2007020793

Table of Contents

NAME That DOG!

What little dog has a big, loud voice? What dog pouts when it is corrected? What dog can squeeze through underground tunnels? What dog can earn thousands of dollars at work? Did you say the dachshund (DOKS-hundt)? Then you are correct!

5

The Badger-Dog

Years ago, people in Europe hunted badgers. These big, furry animals live underground. Hunters often used dogs to track the badgers. The best dogs had short legs and long bodies. They could chase badgers right through their tunnels! The dogs' strong legs could dig through the dirt.

In the 1600s, people in Germany began calling these dogs "dachshunds." The word means "badger-dogs." Germans raised the dogs to hunt badgers and other animals.

The map below shows where Germany is on Earth. The map on the right shows a closer view.

Northern Ireland

Ireland

Great Britain

Atlantic Ocean

North Sea

Norway

Sweden

Denmark

Neth.

Belgium

Lux.

Germany

Poland

Czech

Bay of Biscay

France

Switzerland

Austria

Slovaki

Hungar

Portugal

Slovenia

Croatia

Bosnia And Herz.

Spain

Italy

Mediterranean Sea

7

After a while, there were two sizes of dachshund. The bigger ones hunted badgers. They also hunted wild pigs called *boars*. The smaller ones chased foxes and hares. Both kinds of dachshunds had a great sense of smell. They could follow other animals' **scents**. They could track the animals through forests. They could track them across open fields. They could track them right down into their burrows.

In the 1800s, people brought little dachshunds to the United States. People loved them! Today, dachshunds are very **popular**. In fact, they are America's sixth most popular dog **breed**.

People have all sorts of nicknames for dachshunds. They call them dachsies (DOK-seez), wiener dogs, and sausage dogs.

These smooth-haired dachsies are resting on a sunny day.

Just Like Hot Dogs

Dachshunds have short legs and long bodies. Although they are small, they are very strong. They have deep chests. They have powerful legs for digging.

The dogs come in two sizes—standard and **miniature**. Most standard dachshunds weigh 16 to 32 pounds (7 to 15 kilograms). Many are 8 or 9 inches (20 to 23 centimeters) tall at the shoulder. Miniature dachshunds weigh only about 11 pounds (5 kilograms). They are often only 5 or 6 inches (13 to 15 centimeters) tall at the shoulder!

This standard, smooth-haired dachsie has a shiny coat.

Dachshunds have three different kinds of coats. Smooth-haired dachsies have a short, thick coat. Long-haired dachsies have long, soft fur. It can be straight or a little wavy. Wire-haired dachshunds have hard, straight, wiry hairs. Dachshunds come in just about any color except white. They can be reddish, cream-colored, black, brown, or gray. Some are even spotted.

All dachshunds have long heads and floppy ears. They have dark eyes and smart-looking faces. Their eyebrows go up and down. Their faces seem to show lots of feelings.

Dachsies have lots of energy. They are smart, too. And they are bold and sure of themselves.

Some owners like to dress their wiener dogs in costumes. One outfit is simply a big foam hot-dog bun!

Dachshunds belong to a group of dogs called hounds. Hounds are excellent hunters. They have a good sense of smell. Basset hounds and beagles are hounds, too.

This long-haired dachshund is enjoying a summer day. You can see a wire-haired dachsie on page 19.

A Mind of Its Own

Dachshunds are friendly, loving little dogs. They like to snuggle. They will even burrow under bed covers! They are **loyal** to their owners, too. And most dachsies get along with other pets.

Dachshunds make good pets for adults. They are fine for families with older children. Young children might hurt or trip over these little dogs. And dachshunds sometimes nip at small children, just to protect themselves.

This smooth-haired dachsie loves to be near her family—even when they are swimming!

15

Dachshunds are not for everybody. They can be hard to train. They are certainly smart enough to learn tricks! But they can be hard-headed and stubborn. They sometimes refuse to **obey** their owners.

Dachsies are loud barkers. They often bark at much larger dogs. They also bark at visitors and strangers. Sometimes, their loud barking is a good thing. These dogs make great watchdogs. They notice when something is wrong. Dachshunds have saved their owners from fires and other dangers.

When dachshunds get mad, they stay mad! If you correct them, they pout until they get over it.

Dachshunds have loud voices for such small dogs! Loud barking helps when the dogs go hunting. Owners always know where the dogs are—even when they are underground.

This smooth-haired dachshund is barking at the photographer.

Dachshund Puppies

Most dachshund mothers have three or four puppies in a **litter**. Sometimes they have eight or nine. Each newborn is about as heavy as a lemon. The pups already have long bodies and short legs.

Adult dachshunds have long, narrow heads. But newborns have round heads. Their faces have wrinkles. Their eyes do not open for the first two weeks. The pups stay with their mother. They just want to eat, sleep, and keep warm.

These wire-haired dachshund puppies are drinking their mother's milk.

After about five weeks, the pups move around more. They wander away from their mother. But they do not stay away for long. They still like to be with their family.

As they get older, the pups get braver. They play and run around with their brothers and sisters. That is how they learn to get along with other dogs. They get interested in things around them, too. They go farther away from their mother. By eight weeks, they are ready to be adopted. They are ready to join a new family.

Dachshund puppies eat a lot. At one year, a dachsie weighs 25 times its birth weight!

It is easy to hurt a dachshund puppy's back. You should hold the pup carefully, with both hands. Be careful not to let its back sag!

This wire-
haired dachsie
is just eight
weeks old.

21

Dachshunds Go to Work

Most people keep dachshunds just as pets. They can be wonderful pets! Sometimes they are even heroes. In Oregon, a dachshund named Peter warned his owners of a house fire. The owners got out safely. Peter got an award for his bravery.

Some owners enter their dachshunds in **contests**. In some contests, the dogs show that they are nice looking and well behaved. In others, they show how well they obey **commands**.

These long-haired dachsies are being shown in a contest.

Some dachshunds work for a living instead. They hunt for rare plants called *truffles*. Truffles are sort of like mushrooms. They grow underground, on the roots of trees. They have a special smell. People love how they taste.

People once used pigs to find truffles. Now they use dachshunds. Both pigs and dachshunds can smell truffles easily. Both animals also love to dig. But pigs do not stop digging. They find truffles and tear them up—or even eat them! Dachshunds are much easier to control. And they do not eat the plants. They are the perfect truffle hunters.

People will pay lots of money for truffles. A grocery bag full might sell for $1,000! A good truffle dog can earn thousands of dollars a day.

This smooth-haired dachsie is sniffing a flower—but he will not eat it!

Caring for a Dachshund

Dachshunds make great pets, but they need special care. Their short legs and long backs hold up a lot of weight. These dogs should never jump down from chairs or sofas. Even a short jump can hurt them. They should not run up and down stairs. Sitting up and begging can hurt their backs, too.

Dachshunds do not need much exercise, but they do need some. Staying inside can make them lazy. Then they eat too much and gain weight. Extra weight is hard on a dachshund's back.

This smooth-haired dachsie is enjoying a run through some snow.

When dachshunds go outdoors, they should stay on a leash. They love to chase other animals. If they see a squirrel or rabbit, they might take off. Then they might get lost or hurt.

Dachshunds are easy to keep clean. The smooth-haired dogs are easiest. Owners can just wipe them down with a wet cloth. Long-haired and wire-haired dachsies need **grooming**. Brushing or combing keeps their coats clean and neat.

Healthy dachshunds live to be 14 or 15 years old. And they make their owners very happy!

There are special races for dachshunds. The Wiener Nationals are held in California every year. The dachshunds run along a short track. Thousands of people cheer them on!

This smooth-haired dachsie is curious about the photographer. She has tipped her head to listen!

29

Glossary

breed (BREED) A breed is a certain type of an animal. Dachshunds are a well-known dog breed.

commands (kuh-MANDZ) Commands are orders to do certain things. Sometimes dachshunds do not follow commands.

contests (KON-tests) Contests are meets where people or animals try to win by being the best. People enter some dachshunds in contests.

grooming (GROOM-ing) Grooming an animal is cleaning and brushing it. Long-haired and wire-haired dachshunds need grooming.

litter (LIH-tur) A litter is a group of babies born to one animal at the same time. Dachshund litters often have three or four puppies.

loyal (LOY-ul) To be loyal is to be true to something and stand up for it. Dachshunds are loyal to their owners.

miniature (MIN-ee-uh-chur) Miniature means small for its kind. Some people have miniature dachshunds.

obey (oh-BAY) To obey someone is to do what the person says. Owners can teach their dachshunds to obey them.

popular (PAH-pyuh-lur) When something is popular, it is liked by lots of people. Dachshunds are popular.

scents (SENTS) Scents are smells. Dachshunds love to follow a scent.

To Find Out More

Books to Read

American Kennel Club. *The Complete Dog Book for Kids*. New York: Howell Book House, 1996.

Heyman, Anita. *Gretchen: The Bicycle Dog.* New York: Dutton Children's Books, 2003.

Pinney, Chris. *Dachshunds*. Hauppauge, NY: Barron's Educational Series, 2000.

Stone, Lynn M. *Dachshunds*. Vero Beach, FL: Rourke Publishing, 2003.

Walker, Joan Hustace. *The Everything Dachshund Book: A Complete Guide to Raising, Training, and Caring for Your Dachshund*. Avon, MA: Adams Media Corporation, 2005.

Places to Contact

American Kennel Club (AKC)
Headquarters
260 Madison Ave, New York, NY 10016
Telephone: 212-696-8200

On the Web

Visit our Web site for lots of links about dachshunds:

http://www.childsworld.com/links

Note to Parents, Teachers, and Librarians: We routinely check our Web links to make sure they're safe, active sites—so encourage your readers to check them out!

31

Index

About the Author

Susan H. Gray has a Master's degree in zoology. She has written more than 70 science and reference books for children. She loves to garden and play the piano. Susan lives in Cabot, Arkansas, with her husband Michael and many pets.